THE REVOLUTIONARY WAR

A CHRONOLOGY OF AMERICA'S FIGHT FOR INDEPENDENCE

BY DANIELLE SMITH-LLERA

Consultant:
Nathaniel Sheidley, PhD
Historian and Director of Public History
Bostonian Society
Boston, Massachusetts

CAPSTONE PRESS
a capstone imprint

Connect is published by Capstone Press,
1710 Roe Crest Drive, North Mankato, Minnesota 56003
www.capstonepub.com

Library of Congress Cataloging-in-Publication Data
Smith-Llera, Danielle, 1971–
The revolutionary war : a chronology of America's fight for independence / Danielle
Smith-Llera.
pages cm. — (Connect. The revolutionary war.)
Summary: "Using the chronology text structure, explores how events unfolded
during the Revolutionary War"— Provided by publisher.
Includes bibliographical references and index.
ISBN 978-1-4914-2007-2 (library binding) — ISBN 978-1-4914-2160-4 (pbk.) — ISBN
978-1-4914-2166-6 (ebook pdf)
1. United States—History—Revolution, 1775–1783—Chronology—Juvenile literature.
I. Title.
E208.S66 2015
973.3—dc23   2014026754

Editorial Credits
Jennifer Besel, editor; Veronica Scott, designer; Wanda Winch, media researcher;
    Charmaine Whitman, production specialist

Photo Credits
Bridgeman Images/Peter Newark American Pictures/Private Collection, 20 (bottom),
Peter Newark Pictures/Private Collection, 12, State Historical Society of Wisconsin,
Madison, USA/Edwin W. Deming, 6; Capstone, 41; Courtesy of Army Art Collection,
U.S. Army Center of Military History/H. Charles McBarron, Jr., cover, 26–27; Getty
Images: Ed Vebell, 22, Heritage Images/Guildhall Library & Art Gallery, 7, Stock
Montage, 10–11; Library of Congress: Prints and Photographs Division, 13, 19, 29,
Rare Books and Special Collections Division, 18; National Archives and Records
Administration, ourdocuments.gov, 20 (top); National Park Service, Harpers Ferry
Center/artist Lloyd Kenneth Townsend, 5; North Wind Picture Archives, 25, 31, 33;
Shutterstock: Ekaterina Romanova, ornate scroll design, Ensuper, multi–colored
background, Extezy, vintage calligraphic scroll, f–f–f–f, ornate calligraphy décor
design, Onur Ersin, 43 (top right), wacomka, vintage floral background; SuperStock:
SuperStock, 8–9, 42–43; Thinkstock: Photos.com, 40; U.S. Navy Art Collection,
Washington, D.C., 38–39; www.historicalimagebank.com, painting by Don Troiani,
14–15, 17, 34–35, 37

Printed in the United States of America in Stevens Point, Wisconsin.
092014   008479WZS15

TABLE OF CONTENTS

WAR ON THE HORIZON

Patriot Paul Revere snapped the reins, urging his horse through the night from Boston to Lexington, Massachusetts. He stopped to pound on doors, waking sleeping American colonists to alarming news. More than 650 British soldiers were marching toward Lexington with loaded muskets.

But Great Britain had not always been the colonists' enemy. For more than 100 years, colonists enjoyed being part of the vast British empire. The British government protected the 13 colonies with its navy, the most powerful in the world. Most colonists were proud subjects of King George III. But while the king gave them the freedom to elect their own governments, colonists had no say in British **Parliament**.

But now colonists leaped from their beds to beat drums and clang church bells. About 70 young men snatched up weapons and dashed to Lexington's wide, green lawn in the town center. These were not soldiers, but Minutemen—ordinary people ready to fight at a moment's notice. Dressed in ordinary clothes, these men arranged themselves in rows. They waited. Out of the early morning fog emerged British soldiers in bright red uniforms. It was April 19, 1775. Great Britain and its American colonies were about to go to war.

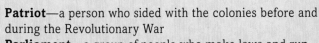

Patriot—a person who sided with the colonies before and during the Revolutionary War
Parliament—a group of people who make laws and run the government in some countries

Leading to Lexington

Twenty years before the events in Lexington, British soldiers and colonists fought side by side on American soil. Their enemy was France and its American Indian **allies**. These groups fought the French and Indian War (1754–1763) for control of North America. In 1763 Great Britain and its American colonies rejoiced at defeating France.

But in London King George III and his ministers could not enjoy the victory for long. They worried about debt. The British government had borrowed a great deal of money during the war to pay soldiers and buy weapons and supplies.

French and Indian soldiers defeated British forces in a battle near what is now Pittsburgh, Pennsylvania. But they could not win the war.

ally—a person or group that gives support

British leaders turned to their American colonies to raise more money. After all, it was expensive for Great Britain to protect the colonies during the war with France.

Great Britain felt it could raise money in its colonies by collecting taxes on goods that were sold there. Taxes made goods more expensive. In 1764 Parliament passed the Sugar Act, which placed a tax on sugar.

Colonists grumbled. Paying taxes that the British government created seemed unfair. Colonists elected their own governments in the colonies, which made their laws and taxes. They had not elected members to Parliament in faraway London.

British leaders debated colonial taxes in the House of Commons in London.

More Taxes

In 1765 Parliament passed the Stamp Act. This law required colonists to pay a tax on printed paper products. Colonists had to pay more for everything from newspapers to playing cards. They were furious. Mobs destroyed British tax collectors' offices. Colonial lawmakers argued the tax was unlawful. Parliament **repealed** the Stamp Act in 1766. But at the same time, it issued an act that said Parliament could pass any laws for the colonies it thought were needed.

Only a year later, Parliament passed the Townshend Acts. These new laws put taxes on products such as glass, paint, and tea arriving on ships from Great Britain.

Many colonists **boycotted** British goods, such as tea, and protested the taxes. Great Britain moved soldiers into towns to protect the tax collectors and end the protests.

When colonists read the Stamp Act, they reacted with angry words and sometimes with violence toward tax collectors.

Fact

News traveled slowly between America and Great Britain. It took at least seven weeks for letters and documents to cross the Atlantic Ocean on a ship. During harsh winter weather, sometimes the flow of mail stopped completely.

repeal—to officially cancel something, such as a law
boycott—to refuse to take part in something as a way of making a protest

Anger Turns to Violence

Anger between colonists and British officials exploded into violence. On the cold night of March 5, 1770, colonists in Boston, Massachusetts, hurled snowballs and rocks at British soldiers. The soldiers fired their guns in defense. Five colonists died in what became known as the Boston Massacre. Later that year Parliament repealed all the Townshend taxes except for the one on tea.

Tempers cooled briefly after that. Colonists continued to ask for representation in Parliament. But the British government wouldn't budge. Soon the anger boiled again. On December 16, 1773, at least 50 colonists boarded three British ships in Boston Harbor. They broke open containers and poured more than 90,000 pounds (45 tons) of tea into the water. Today that much tea would be worth almost $1 million. The British found this "Boston Tea Party" unforgivable.

Patriots began calling the shootings in Boston a "massacre." Using that word made it sound like the British had killed hundreds of people without care, even though that's not what happened.

Parliament punished Boston for destroying the tea by passing several new, strict laws. The colonists called them the Intolerable Acts. In March 1774 the British closed the city's busy harbor until colonists paid for the destroyed tea. In May a British military general took control of Massachusetts' government.

People in other colonies were afraid Great Britain would take over their governments too. They rushed to organize themselves. On September 5, 1774, **delegates** from all the colonies except Georgia gathered for the Continental Congress in Philadelphia.

The delegates crafted a petition to King George. They tried to persuade him to lift the painful Intolerable Acts. If the king did not, they threatened to boycott all British goods.

The king ignored the letter. Six months after the Continental Congress first met, British soldiers and Minutemen faced off outside Boston on the Lexington green.

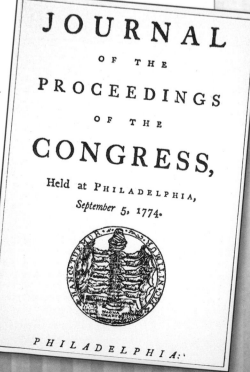

JOURNAL OF THE PROCEEDINGS OF THE CONGRESS, Held at PHILADELPHIA, September 5, 1774.

PHILADELPHIA:

Delegates to the First Continental
Congress met at Carpenter's Hall
in Philadelphia.

delegate—someone who represents other people
at a meeting

WAR BEGINS

The small group of Minutemen in Lexington stood firmly before the larger group of British soldiers. Both sides eyed each other tensely. Suddenly someone fired a shot. Then muskets fired from both sides. Minutes later eight Patriots lay dead. The rest fled home.

Feeling confident, British soldiers marched into nearby Concord. They searched the town for hidden weapons. Meanwhile, news of the battle at Lexington spread through nearby towns. Several hundred **militiamen** gathered outside Concord. They fired shots at British soldiers defending a bridge leading to the town.

Outnumbered and exhausted from the long day of traveling and fighting, the British began the march back to Boston. But the fighting was not over. All along the road, Patriots shot at them from behind trees and stone walls. By the end of the day, more than 250 British soldiers were wounded, killed, or missing. The Patriots lost fewer than 100 men.

In the following days, as many 20,000 colonial militiamen traveled to the countryside outside of Boston. They blocked roads to prevent the British from traveling out of Boston. Yet the British would not be so easily trapped. Their warships docked freely in the harbor, delivering more soldiers and weapons.

Fact

The British soldiers did not go to Lexington to start war. Their orders were to hunt for weapons and gunpowder stored there by the colonists. They also planned to capture Patriots who were leading the rebellion against Great Britain.

militiamen—a group of volunteer citizens who serve as soldiers in emergencies

The Fight for Boston

The Second Continental Congress met in Philadelphia on May 10, 1775. Delegates from all 13 colonies were losing hope of making peace with Great Britain. On June 14, they created the Continental army and named George Washington its commander.

A few days later, British soldiers rowed ashore near Boston and marched toward a hill. Americans, hiding on the hill behind dirt mounds, had little gunpowder for their muskets. They waited to fire until the British soldiers were upon them.

Then the Patriots suddenly fired. Many British soldiers fell. Surprised by the furious attack, the rest of the army retreated. But when the Patriots ran out of gunpowder, they fled. The British won the Battle of Bunker Hill. Yet it was a costly victory. More than 1,000 British soldiers were killed or wounded. The colonists had proven they would not be defeated easily.

On July 3, 1775, Washington officially took control of the army. This tall, quiet man was a wealthy farmer and member of the Continental Congress. He had led a small group of soldiers during the French and Indian War. But little could prepare him for leading untrained men with few supplies against a powerful army.

Patriots waited behind dirt mounds for the British to come close during the Battle of Bunker Hill.

African-Americans Fight for Freedom

African-American slaves fought on both sides of the war. White owners often sent slaves to fight in their places. Washington's Continental army was a mixture of white and African-American soldiers.

In November 1775 the British promised slaves freedom if they ran away from their masters to join the British. Many slaves did. After the war ended, many African-Americans were given freedom. However others were sold back into slavery.

Even though fighting had begun, the Continental Congress tried one last time to make peace with Great Britain. On July 8, 1775, delegates sent a letter to King George. In this "Olive Branch Petition," they promised that the colonies only wanted fairer taxes. They did not wish to leave the British empire.

The king responded by sending more soldiers to Boston. He also offered to pay men from Germany to fight the colonists. At least 30,000 **Hessians** accepted the offer.

Throughout that fall and winter, fighting between American and British forces broke out from Canada down to the British-held Bahamas. A short book, published in January 1776, inspired more colonists to dream of a new nation. Thomas Paine's *Common Sense* convinced many colonists to fight for independence from the British.

Hessian—a German soldier hired by the British

Two months after Paine's book came out, Washington proved that colonists could win their freedom. For months Boston had been caught in a tug-of-war between British and American fighters. During the night of March 4, 1776, Washington ordered that weapons be hauled high above the city. The British were shocked to awake to cannon pointing down at them from Dorchester Heights. Within a few days, the British army sailed out of Boston.

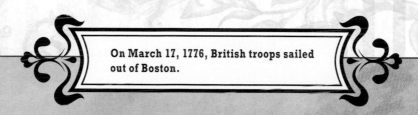

On March 17, 1776, British troops sailed out of Boston.

REBELLION TO REVOLUTION

On July 2 Congress took a bold step toward independence. Delegates voted to declare the 13 colonies free from Great Britain. On July 4, 1776, they adopted the Declaration of Independence. Written by Congressman Thomas Jefferson, the declaration stated that all men had rights and even a king could not take these rights away.

Declaration of Independence

By signing the Declaration, American leaders became British traitors.

Americans were now fighting a revolution to end British rule in the colonies. General Washington made sure the Declaration was read to his soldiers. He hoped it would explain why they were fighting.

After driving the British out of Boston, Washington knew the enemy was aiming for another major port. He hustled most of the Continental army to New York City. But Washington was worried. His soldiers were inexperienced. And Congress sent only a trickle of supplies and weapons to his 19,000 men.

Meanwhile, more than 400 British ships filled New York Harbor, defending the city built on an island. They could easily deliver soldiers and supplies to its shores. Soon 32,000 British soldiers arrived, led by British General William Howe.

Battling Smallpox

For the colonists, smallpox proved to be a more deadly enemy than the British. British soldiers carried this disease to the colonies. When the revolution began, colonists gathered for meetings or protests. The disease spread quickly through the crowds.

By 1775 smallpox had spread through Boston. In May 1776 smallpox had infected half of the Americans fighting the British in Canada.

In 1777 Washington ordered that each soldier receive a tiny dose of the smallpox virus. After this treatment most soldiers survived if they caught the disease.

Struggling Americans

Washington arranged his soldiers and guns along the roads and high ground on Long Island, outside of New York City. Then they waited.

Crossing the Delaware River in the winter was hard and dangerous. But the work paid off when they were able to surprise the enemy.

But on August 27, 1776, General Howe found an unguarded road. He surprised the Americans by attacking them from behind. It was a devastating defeat for the Americans. They lost about 1,000 of the nearly 10,000 men who fought the battle. The British lost 400 of their 20,000 men. Washington and his surviving army escaped in boats during the night.

That fall the Continental army lost more battles around New York. Finally, Washington led his small, ragged army south through New Jersey and into Delaware. He needed a win.

Washington made a daring move on Christmas night. He and 2,400 men rowed across the icy Delaware River. In driving snow they marched to Trenton, New Jersey. The next morning they caught a group of Hessians by surprise.

The Hessians scrambled for weapons. But Washington's men surrounded the town. When the Americans killed the Hessians' leader, the Hessian soldiers lost courage and fled. The Americans captured nearly 1,000 of them, along with needed weapons.

Fact

Some American soldiers used rifles. These rifles were more accurate than British muskets. Tiny grooves inside the rifle barrels made bullets spin. This spin helped bullets fly straighter.

British Plan to End the War

The British were shocked by their defeat in Trenton. They sent 8,000 soldiers under General Charles Cornwallis to New Jersey. On January 2, 1777, Washington got word that the British were planning to cross a river to raid his camp the next morning. He made a plan of his own.

That night the Americans left campfires burning and slipped away. Cornwallis' army awoke to find Washington's camp empty. Meanwhile, Washington's men surprised the British in nearby Princeton. The outnumbered British soldiers fled or surrendered.

Washington's army camped in Morristown, New Jersey, for the rest of the winter. Meanwhile British General John Burgoyne formed a plan for ending the war. He urged Great Britain to take control of New York's Hudson River Valley. This wide river flowed through New York and down to New York City harbor. The Continental army transported people and goods on the river. Burgoyne hoped by taking control of the river, the troublesome northern colonies would be cut off from the southern ones.

Battle of Princeton, New Jersey

That summer Burgoyne sailed south from Canada and marched toward the Hudson River Valley. General Howe was supposed to march north from New York City and meet up with him. But against orders, Howe sailed south to attack Philadelphia.

Battle of Saratoga

Washington rushed to block Howe's army from reaching Philadelphia, America's capital at the time. But on September 11, 1777, Howe attacked Washington's army of 16,000 soldiers near Brandywine Creek. Before night fell the British killed, wounded, or captured nearly 1,000 Americans. Washington could not stop Howe from marching on toward Philadelphia.

Meanwhile, Burgoyne desperately needed help in New York. But Howe was too far away. Burgoyne's men hauled heavy weapons and supply wagons through the wilderness. Militia shot at them from behind trees.

Burgoyne crossed the Hudson River near Saratoga, New York, with his hungry and exhausted men. But American Major General Horatio Gates and his men were waiting on the other bank.

Burgoyne's and Gates' armies faced each other on September 19, 1777. Bullets whizzed from the American side. Colonel Daniel Morgan's 500 trained riflemen shot many British officers. The British soldiers were alarmed to lose so many leaders at the beginning of the battle. Hessians arrived to fight, and the British claimed the battlefield. Yet Burgoyne lost 600 men. His army was shrinking.

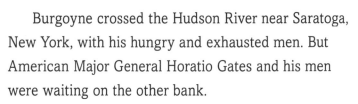

American soldiers often used their knowledge of the land to surprise the British, including during the Battle of Saratoga.

British Lose the North

Howe captured Philadelphia on September 26, 1777. However, Burgoyne's army was losing its grip on New York. Thousands of militia joined General Gates' army. In a second Battle of Saratoga, Gates positioned his men on Bemis Heights. This hill overlooked the road the British needed to travel onward. Burgoyne's men were trapped and outnumbered.

On October 7 Burgoyne's men tried to fight their way out. Rifle shots crackled. American Major General Benedict Arnold boldly led attacks from horseback. Finally, Burgoyne and his men escaped to a nearby fort. Gates' men surrounded the fort. Burgoyne waited for help to arrive. But it never came.

On October 17 Burgoyne handed his sword to Gates in a symbol of surrender. Great Britain had lost its power in the northern states. American Patriots rejoiced.

News of Burgoyne's surrender traveled across the Atlantic Ocean. France had lost land in North America to the British in the French and Indian War. Upon hearing of Britain's defeat, the French joyously celebrated. King Louis XIV had not believed the Americans could defeat the British—until then. France agreed to join the war to help the Americans win.

Burgoyne, left center, surrendered to Gates after the second Battle of Saratoga. The surrender was a big loss for the British.

A Long, Cold Winter

On February 6, 1778, France signed an agreement to fight alongside the Americans until they won independence from Great Britain. But this hopeful news traveled slowly. Washington and the Continental army fought to survive the bitter winter as they camped outside Philadelphia. There in Valley Forge the soldiers' greatest enemy was cold and hunger. Washington wrote to Congress, demanding more supplies for his desperate men. But little arrived. Many soldiers had no shoes, coats, or blankets. The 11,000 men ate only flour and some salted meat. Washington feared his soldiers would die or abandon him.

But Washington refused to give up. He spent the winter training his army. He selected Baron Friedrich von Steuben, an experienced soldier from Prussia, to train his men. Von Steuben taught the men to stay organized during battles. He also trained them to use **bayonets** like the British.

Finally in May 1778, news of the **alliance** with France reached Valley Forge. Washington's men fired their guns in celebration. Help was on the way.

bayonet—a long metal blade attached to the end of a musket or rifle
alliance—an agreement between groups to work together

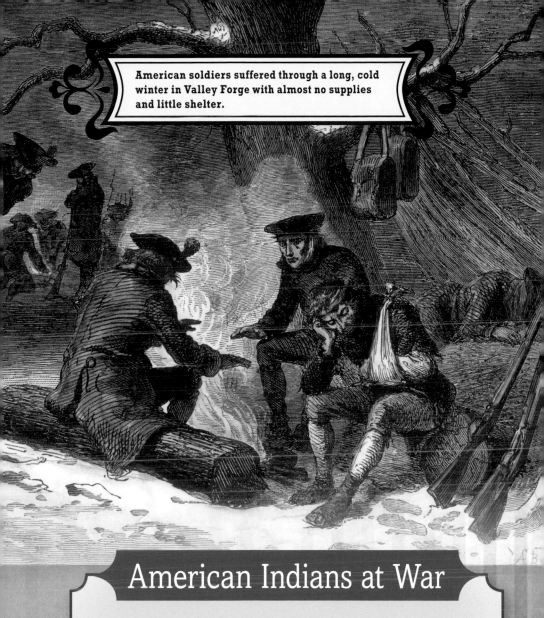

American soldiers suffered through a long, cold winter in Valley Forge with almost no supplies and little shelter.

American Indians at War

Most American Indians did not want to get involved in the American Revolution. However, they also feared that colonists would push them off their lands if they took control of the land. When Great Britain promised to protect Indian land, most groups sided with the British. Washington resented that Iroquois tribes were helping the British. In 1779 he ordered his soldiers to burn Iroquois' homes and destroy their crops.

THE WAR SHIFTS SOUTH

After Burgoyne's surrender in Saratoga, the British changed their strategy. They wanted **Loyalists** to help them win the war. Many Loyalists lived in the southern colonies of Virginia, Georgia, North Carolina, and South Carolina. So the British refocused their plan on the south.

On June 18, 1778, the British moved out of Philadelphia. But they had plans to take over important port cities in the south. On December 29, 1778, a force of British soldiers, Loyalists, and Hessians traveled across swampy Georgia. They surprised the fewer than 900 American fighters defending Savannah.

The small American force was no match for the British force of around 3,000 troops. They retreated, and the British captured Savannah. British ships could then easily dock and deliver supplies and soldiers.

In May 1780 British ships confidently sailed to Charleston, South Carolina. The Continental army of the south was based in this important port city. British General Henry Clinton trapped the American soldiers. The British took control of all roads leaving the city. British naval ships in the harbor prevented escape over water.

Loyalist—a colonist who was loyal to Great Britain during the Revolutionary War

For days Americans fought desperately to hold Charleston. But they were forced to surrender on May 12, 1780. The British took 5,000 American prisoners. They also captured three warships—most of America's navy. To Americans' dismay, Great Britain now had firm control over the southern colonies.

British soldiers trapped the Americans during the Siege of Charleston.

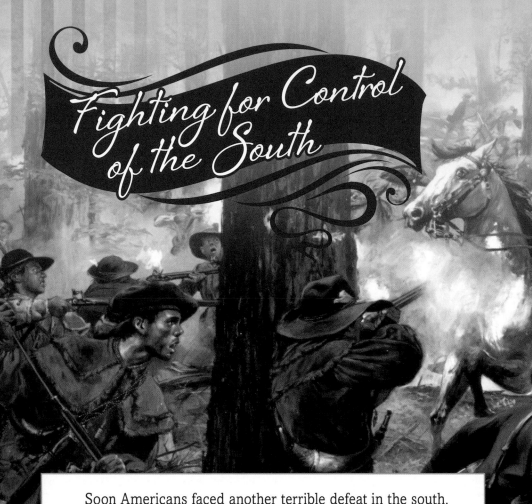

Fighting for Control of the South

Soon Americans faced another terrible defeat in the south. Congress had sent General Gates, who defeated Burgoyne in Saratoga, to the south. On August 16, 1780, he led exhausted soldiers in attacking a British fort in Camden, South Carolina. British General Cornwallis' army of well-trained soldiers and Loyalists killed or wounded nearly 1,000 Americans and took nearly 1,000 more prisoner.

Despite their victories Great Britain soon found fighting in the American countryside a challenge. On October 7, 1780, Patriot militia surrounded British Major Patrick Ferguson and a group of Loyalist fighters in South Carolina. In a bloody battle on the top of King's Mountain, the Patriots shot and captured nearly all the Loyalists.

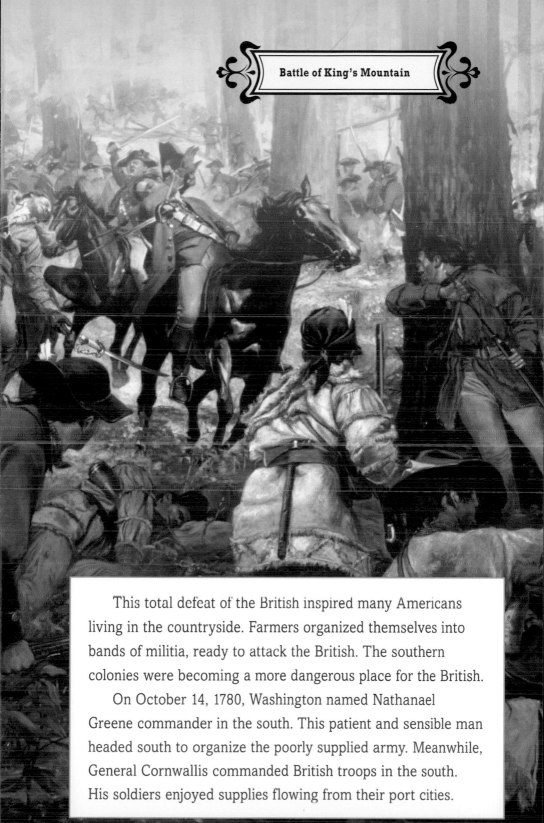

This total defeat of the British inspired many Americans living in the countryside. Farmers organized themselves into bands of militia, ready to attack the British. The southern colonies were becoming a more dangerous place for the British.

On October 14, 1780, Washington named Nathanael Greene commander in the south. This patient and sensible man headed south to organize the poorly supplied army. Meanwhile, General Cornwallis commanded British troops in the south. His soldiers enjoyed supplies flowing from their port cities.

Finding British Weaknesses

Greene planned to weaken the British before fighting them in battle. He divided his army into smaller groups, which spread far into the countryside. The British followed them. When the British soldiers were far from their port cities, fewer supplies could reach them.

Greene also welcomed the help of militiamen living in the countryside. With their help he could use **guerilla warfare**. In this kind of fighting, small groups of fighters attacked larger groups of soldiers by surprise.

Greene's officer Brigadier General Daniel Morgan lured British General Banastre Tarleton's soldiers into the countryside of South Carolina. On January 17, 1781, Morgan waited in a wooded area used for cattle grazing called Cowpens. Tarleton's men attacked. Morgan's riflemen shot down the British officers. Tarleton retreated, leaving Morgan with nearly 900 captured British soldiers.

guerilla warfare—a type of military action using small groups of fighters to carry out surprise attacks against enemy forces

Greene's army of more than 4,000 soldiers lured Cornwallis' army far into the North Carolina countryside. The Americans halted in the forested hills of Guilford Courthouse. Cornwallis' nearly 2,000 men attacked on January 17, 1781. American riflemen hid behind trees and shot many British.

After killing or wounding more than 500 British men, Greene retreated. He had lost 250 men and did not want to lose more. Cornwallis hustled his army back toward the coast. He was in desperate need of supplies.

The Battle of Cowpens was a great victory for the Continental army in the south.

Battle of Yorktown

Cornwallis had lost too many men in the Carolinas. He marched away from Greene's army and north toward Virginia's Chesapeake Bay. In the summer of 1781, Cornwallis settled his army at Yorktown, Virginia.

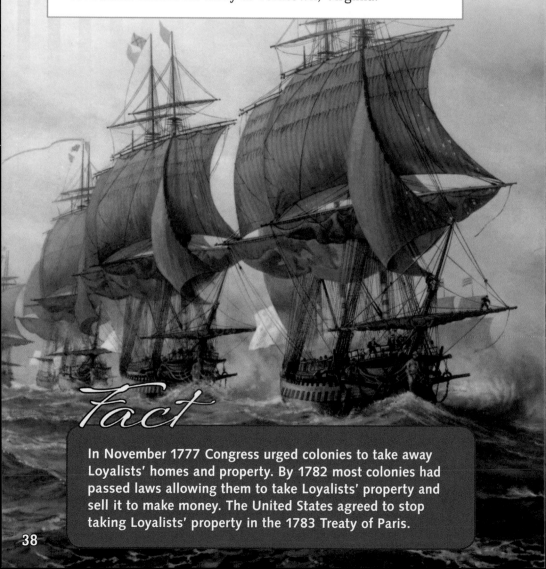

Fact

In November 1777 Congress urged colonies to take away Loyalists' homes and property. By 1782 most colonies had passed laws allowing them to take Loyalists' property and sell it to make money. The United States agreed to stop taking Loyalists' property in the 1783 Treaty of Paris.

Cornwallis believed his army of around 8,000 soldiers was safe on the Yorktown peninsula. The British navy patrolled the waters. But Cornwallis did not know that Washington and his army were marching from New York to Virginia. He also didn't know that French warships were racing toward them.

On September 5, 1781, French and British warships met in the Chesapeake Bay. They fired cannon at each other for more than two hours. Six British ships were badly damaged in the Battle of the Chesapeake. The battered British navy sailed away to New York for repairs.

Washington saw his chance to trap Cornwallis. He marched about 17,000 American and French soldiers into Yorktown. By late September they had completely surrounded Cornwallis' army. The French navy blocked escape by sea.

On September 28, 1781, the defining battle of the American Revolution began. Guns and cannon fired both day and night for days. Soldiers on both sides fired at each other while hiding in trenches.

PEACE COMES SLOWLY

Cornwallis' army in Yorktown was trapped and outnumbered by the Americans. No British ships arrived to help. One night Cornwallis and his men tried to escape the peninsula in boats. But a storm drove them back to Yorktown.

Finally, Cornwallis gave up. On October 17, 1781, he sent an officer lifting a white flag of surrender onto the battlefield. Two days later he sent an officer to deliver his sword to American and French commanders. The Americans took his entire army prisoner.

Against tradition, Cornwallis did not go in person to surrender. He sent his sword with one of his officers (left) to the American camp.

For the next two years, fighting continued. But there was no progress, and the war was in a stalemate.

The British government grew impatient. However, it wasn't eager to sign a treaty giving the United States independence. Parliament offered the colonies more freedoms—but as part of the British empire. The Americans refused.

MAJOR BATTLES OF THE REVOLUTION

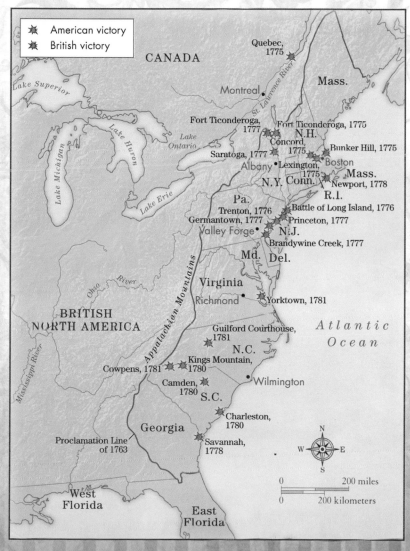

A New Nation

Almost a year after the surrender at Yorktown, leaders from the United States and Great Britain struggled to write an agreement. Finally on September 3, 1783, the Treaty of Paris was signed. In the document Great Britain accepted that the 13 colonies were part of an independent nation.

But this new nation was poor. The states were in debt after the long, expensive war. And the new nation was disorganized. Each state printed its own money and made its own laws. They behaved more like independent states than a united country.

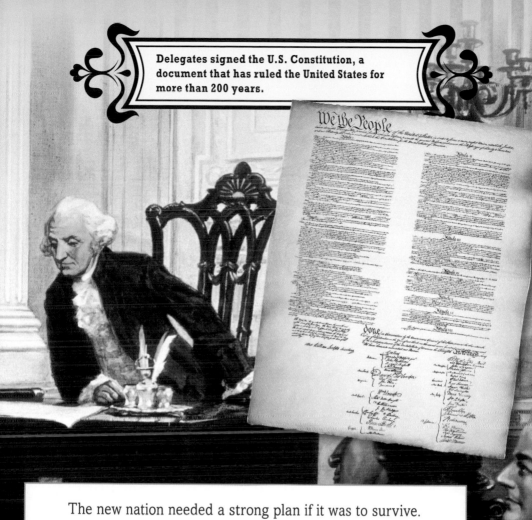

Delegates signed the U.S. Constitution, a document that has ruled the United States for more than 200 years.

We the People

The new nation needed a strong plan if it was to survive. In May 1787 delegates from the states met at the Constitutional Convention. Leaders fiercely debated how to organize the new government. They wrote their plan, and the U.S. Constitution was born. On September 17 the delegates voted to accept the document. The states then had to accept or reject the new constitution. On July 2, 1788, the ninth state accepted the document, and the Constitution became the law of the land.

The new United States and Great Britain teetered on the edge of war for years. They would go to war again in 1812. However, Americans would continue to defend and protect the independence they had won—a freedom that exists today.

TIMELINE

1763
The French and Indian War ends.

1765
Parliament passes the Stamp Act. Colonists protest the taxes.

1767
Parliament passes the Townshend Acts.

1768
British troops arrive in Boston to enforce laws.

1770
Five colonists are killed in the Boston Massacre.

1773
Colonists dump tea into Boston Harbor.

1774
Parliament passes the Intolerable Acts.

The First Continental Congress meets in Philadelphia.

April 1775
War begins with a short battle in Lexington, Massachusetts.

May 1775
The Second Continental Congress meets.

June 1775
The British win at the Battle of Bunker Hill.

July 1775
The Continental Congress sends Great Britain the Olive Branch Petition.

July 1776

Congress adopts the Declaration of Independence.

August 1776

Americans are defeated in the Battle of Long Island, New York.

December 1776

Washington defeats Hessians in the Battle of Trenton, New Jersey.

September 1777

The British capture Philadelphia.

October 1777

Burgoyne surrenders after the Battles of Saratoga.

February 1778

Americans sign the Treaty of Alliance with France.

June 1778

The British give up Philadelphia.

December 1778

The British capture Savannah, Georgia.

1780

The British capture Charleston, South Carolina.

January 1781

Americans defeat the British at Cowpens, South Carolina.

March 1781

The British win the Battle of Guilford Courthouse, North Carolina.

October 1781

British General Cornwallis surrenders at Yorktown, Virginia.

1783

The United States and Great Britain sign the Treaty of Paris.

1788

The United States officially adopts the Constitution.

GLOSSARY

alliance (uh-LY-uhnts)—an agreement between groups to work together

ally (AL-eye)—a person or group that gives support

bayonet (BAY-uh-net)—a long metal blade attached to the end of a musket or rifle

boycott (BOY-kot)—to refuse to take part in something as a way of making a protest

delegate (DEL-uh-guht)—someone who represents other people at a meeting

guerrilla warfare (gur-RIL-lah WOR-fair)—a type of military action using small groups of fighters to carry out surprise attacks against enemy forces

Hessian (HE-shun)—a German soldier hired by the British

Loyalist (LOI-uh-list)—a colonist who was loyal to Great Britain during the Revolutionary War

militiamen (muh-LISH-uh MEN)—a group of volunteer citizens who serve as soldiers in emergencies

Parliament (PAR-luh-muhnt)—a group of people who make laws and run the government in some countries

Patriot (PAY-tree-uht)—a person who sided with the colonies before and during the Revolutionary War

repeal (ri-PEEL)—to officially cancel something, such as a law

READ MORE

Gunderson, Jessica. *A Rebel Among Redcoats: A Revolutionary War Novel*. The Revolutionary War. North Mankato, Minn.: Stone Arch Books, 2015.

Huey, Lois Miner. *Voices of the American Revolution: Stories from the Battlefields*. Voices of War. North Mankato, Minn.: Capstone Press, 2011.

Morey, Allan. *A Timeline History of the Declaration of Independence*. Timeline Trackers: America's Beginnings. Minneapolis: Lerner Publications, 2014.

CRITICAL THINKING USING THE COMMON CORE

1. Compare Nathanael Greene's warfare tactics with the way the British army fought. Why were Greene's tactics so effective against the British? Use other sources to support your answer.
   (Integration of Knowledge and Ideas)

2. On March 5, 1770, five colonists who had been throwing snowballs and rocks at British soldiers were killed. Patriots called the event the "Boston Massacre." Look up the word "massacre" in a dictionary, and compare that definition to what happened in Boston that night. Was the event a massacre? Why would Patriots use that word to describe the event?
   (Craft and Structure)

INTERNET SITES

FactHound offers a safe, fun way to find Internet sites related to this book. All of the sites on FactHound have been researched by our staff.

Here's all you do:

Visit *www.facthound.com*

Type in this code: 9781491420072

INDEX